Unlinear

a make-belief word for very real poems

Mrinaal Sehgal

Made with ❤ on the BookLeaf Publishing Platform

www.bookleafpub.in

www.bookleafpub.com

Dedication

To Mum and Dad,
So much comes and goes but the two of you always seem
to have my back.

Preface

Life is full of paradoxes and polarities which are often incomprehensible to us in their entirety. A trauma or an abuse survivor could be brimming with hope, a woman raging against archaic patriarchal structures could still deeply believe in fairytales, and you might truly understand the magnitude of your strength while you're down on your knees. You could love God so much that you might fight hard with them and refuse to acknowledge their presence for a while. Alternatively, you could hate or judge a human so much that you think by trying to show love and compassion towards them, you can change their nature. Oftentimes, we are quick to embrace one side of ourselves and completely ignore the other. Perhaps this deep dismissal stems from our interaction with language where the words, syntax, and other grammatical structures are so clearly defined that we seek to superimpose this clarity on the very things they were created to express. Even before we have fully felt the extent of what we are going through or who we are, we are quick to slot ourselves into boxes and identities often negating the potential of everything else we could be. Our history as mankind is demarcated into periods, our poetry slotted into sections, our collective faith divided into religions, our lifetime into years and so much more.

The word 'Unlinear' is a very conscious choice to title this book because it's not an actual word but rather serves as a subtle slight to the perfection of language that often holds us back from fully facing the raw unintelligible mess of our human existence. The subtitle 'a make-belief word for very real poems' hints at the overwhelming presence of opposites in both life and in this collection. As the title suggests, this book follows no apparent structure in terms of how the poems are placed and in fact, a poem about pure romantic hope may immediately follow one highlighting deep existential despair. This is because our journey of evolution and healing is never linear. A very bad moment can ruin a perfectly good day or old memories can come to haunt us when we've long forgotten about them. Certain poems have two versions in the book showing us that we can be two very different people in different moments and can have a very varying perspective on the same theme at different points in our life.

 As a poet, I've been guilty of playing with fancy words and challenging rhyming schemes to deflect the truth of what I'm truly going through. However, over time I'm slowly coming to realise that true poetry is so much more than just words. It is honesty. It is love. And it is everything else that comes with fully standing in your integrity and truth, no matter how many times you fear

rejection or hurt. Writing these pieces allowed me to unbox, unravel, undo all my preconceived ideas of who I was and liberated me into expressing and feeling everything else I could be and I could feel.
I hope that, in reading them, you too are tinged with a similar sense of exploration and liberation.

Acknowledgements

I think the biggest fear that ever came with me writing a book was that the acknowledgments would probably run longer than the book itself. The universe and life has been exceptionally kind in sending such amazing people and opportunities my way that my words will fall short in expressing the true extent of my gratitude. However, as a writer I must still try.

Firstly, to the people this book is dedicated to. The dedication really sums it all. I know it sounds clichéd but if it wasn't for the both of you, I would not be me.

To Tiddi and her Puttu, thank you for reaffirming my faith in love when it was hanging by a thread.

To Mani and her Chirag, ditto. (If this isn't pressure for the two of you to end up together, I don't know what else is)

To sisters who are like friends and friends who are like sisters—Jahnwhee, Zee, Vedu, Marisha, Akanksha, Soumya and so many many more. Thank you for being my partners-in-crime, for always looking out for me, and for simply being you.

To Zaid and Hamza, my brothers from other mothers who've always had my back, regardless of the circumstance.

To Mamu-Mami, and to Jaya Aunty-Prem Uncle, thank

you so much for restoring my faith in non-biological parents when I honestly had none left. Your love is so kind and healing that I will forever be grateful.

To Dadi and Nani, the most powerful matriarchs I've ever seen even if sometimes, you don't feel that way. You will always be a source of inspiration to me.

To Dadu and Nanu, you may not physically be here with me but your blood will always course through my veins. These pieces are a testament to that.

To the army of uncles and aunties, who've always been behind me in so many different capacities as family friends, mentors, healers, older partners-in-crime, and so much more. This does not include the gossipy ones, of course.

To all the people who've stood by me like a rock in the past couple of months and have been there for me in the strongest and most practical way possible. Especially, Sofi, Sugandha, Anshuka Aunty, Sajal, and Mayank. Thank you so much for everything you've all done for me.

To all my school teachers for the roots, and to all my college professors for wings. What you all do matters so much.

To Book Leaf Publishing, for helping me get over my misguided fear of the red-tape behind publishing and making the process so effortlessly easy. Thank you for creating a platform that let me solely focus on the writing.

To Manoj Uncle, thank you for getting me back to writing a couple of years ago. If I hadn't started writing for you, I would not have been able to write these pieces. Lastly, to all the angels and pantheons of Gods and Goddesses who have always looked out for me, thank you for protecting me, guiding me and holding me through the darkest of my times. My words will always be yours.

To everybody I've ever crossed paths with, know that in your own way—kindly or fiercely, minutely or massively, you've all taught me something and for that I will always be eternally grateful.

1. I Don't Know How to Write Anymore.

When I was a cute little child,
Writing was so easy
And my poetry so soothingly mild.

I learnt new words,
Strung them together just fine.
The stylistic meters were borrowed
But the poems all mine.

Meticulously, I honed my craft
And for ages and ages,
I sat on the draft.

In earnest patience,
I waited for the perfect season,
When I would morph into the perfect poet
Whose works fit well within reason.

Then true feelings came into play,
Overcame all logic,
And simply took my words away.

Now, as a writer

I just try not to sink.
I don't write anymore,
I bleed with my ink.

And bleeding is very painful,
Haemorrhaging even more so.
So should the evidence of this
Really be shared with the world?
I honestly don't know.

My emotions no longer fit
Into perfect rhymes,
And I'm also afraid I'm slightly
Running out of time.
Just like in life,
My poems are searching for the perfect ending
But man, I just can't get that last line.

2. Tsunami

So did the earth finally crumble
Under this ocean of tears,
Shattered by the weight
Its chest had borne for so many years?

Or was there a sudden attack
On the gentle heart of the moon?
A broken heartbeat that once made
Each wave dance to its mystical tune.

Flowers that bloom so punctually
Season after season,
Drowned before they could wilt
For no apparent reason.

The master of earthly cycles
Suddenly snatches everything before its time.
Nature violates its own harmony,
And we're just supposed to be fine?

3. The Hermit by the Sea I

When you leave everything
To become a hermit by the sea,
Then there is deep wisdom in abandoning
All hopes of finding the words you've waited to hear
Your entire life make their way to you in a
Forgotten, floating glass bottle.
Don't look at the seas for ships
Carrying the strangers you once used to love
And maybe will always do.
Instead,
Allow the tides and the moon to teach you
True lessons about the universe.
About the transience of everything.
You took to the distant seas
As a poultice for your wounds,
But always, always, always remember—
It is in the nature of salt to sting.

4. The Hermit by the Sea II

The hermit by the sea,
The girl who just wants to be.
Why fight for the big when you're happy with the small?
Why find the right words when you can say none at all?
Why settle for just a little bit of love when you promised yourself more?
Why drown yourself in the ocean when your fairytale awaits at the shore?

5. Rust

Is what will set in your bones
As you try to shed off the weight of your marriage
While simultaneously trying to
Survive the divorce.

Rust
Is the colour of the saree
That your friends will pool in together
To gift you at your wedding.
The blouse however will be snatched by your mother-in-
law
To show you your true place.
That no matter what you built in your marriage,
Nothing was ever truly yours
If you ever choose to break away.

Rust
Will be the taste of blood in your mouth
As you bite your cheek in anger
When you realise that the pain is not about losing
Something as small as a blouse
But rather what it sheathed;
Your dignity.

Rust
Is what has gathered on old metal trunks
Hiding history and mythology books
That teach you the cyclical fate of women.
That while we are too busy safeguarding ourselves from
men,
We often forget,
Women also hurt other women.
And they do it better.

6. True Writer's Block

Time and time again,
You've subtly made me feel like I'm not truly a writer.
You see, compared to big business tycoons,
Our pockets are considerably lighter.
But no matter what anyone implies,
The love and truth in our hearts will always shine
brighter.
And even if these poems end up proving nothing,
They'll at least prove I'm a fighter.

7. What's in a Name?

When I was growing up,
I was led to believe that
Names carve out your destiny.
If your name meant it,
Magically you'd transform into being pretty,
Or as my sister puts it, 'simply lucky'.

I once loved a boy
With a constant frown.
His name reminded me
Of a starry proper noun.
I soon found out that his name had another meaning,
One that simply left me gleaming,
As I thought to myself,
"Oh yay! anchors help you ground."
Little did I know then,
Anchors can also make you drown.

There is no moral to this story.
Simply that romanticism can also be gory.
Every single thing has two sides—
Names, metaphors, even ocean tides.

There is no point in getting stuck to one,
If you don't acknowledge the shadow,
You'll never fully comprehend the sun.

8. Spring Flowers

One day,
I woke up in a lot of pain.
So much so that I begged God
To take me away.
But like any dear loved one—
He sent me spring flowers
To make my day.
Really,
Sometimes it takes so little
To make our minds sway.

9. Pale Pink Ashes

The sea sweeps beyond the horizon,
To infinities we can't see
And washes away the remnants of us,
The ghosts of you and me.
The sun dips beyond the horizon
To the depths we couldn't be
And darkens the outlines of us,
The shadows of you and me.
The sky extends beyond the horizon,
So many illusions seen so clearly.
One of these, the likes of us,
The traces of you and me.

That glow belongs to the horizon,
And yet transgresses every boundary
To reach the fragments of us,
The chalk dust of you and me.
That hope belongs to the horizon
And touches everything that is meant to be.
Except the tragedy of us,
The sad story of you and me.
That breeze belongs to the horizon,
And sways oh-so-gently,
Taking with it the tale of us,

The unfinished legend of you and me.

Somethings belong to the horizon.
Somewhere, so do we.
Somethings go beyond the horizon.
Somewhere, so do we.
Somethings we don't know about the horizon.
Neither do we about you and me.
The sea sweeps, the sun sets, and the sky rolls,
All that we can see.
The hope glows and the breeze blows,
All that we can feel.
And all of these end up scattering,
On every broken story,
The pale pink ashes of you and me.

10. Pale Pink Lotuses

In my long, never-ending search for you,
I stumble upon the pale pink ashes of our story.
All of a sudden, another cosmic play begins anew.

I collect every single remnant from the undone knots of
destiny,
And after taking God's name,
Plant them in the haunted graveyard of your memory.

The faint moonlight pierces through the veil of tragedy,
And shows me the faded outline,
of a long-forgotten promise of the most breathtaking
eternity.

As symbols of a love so pure and true,
Out of thin air,
Our pale pink lotuses suddenly grew.
And when our time comes, my love—
I will finally offer these to you.

The rolling sea that separates us tried to drown them.
But in the abyss of its depths,
They learnt how to produce a pearl.
The breeze tried to carry them with whispers of hope.

But loyal to their watery ground,
They blossomed whorl by whorl.
Still they stand, laughing in the face of the raging sun
Whose blaze seeks to serve as their pyre.
Because unlike all other flowers,
Our lotuses know how to bloom in the fire.

11. Mischief Maker

You may read these poems,
And feel very deeply that they are about you.
But from the bottom of my heart,
I want you to know that's not true.
They're about someone else I once knew.

If anybody else thinks they are that someone,
That will also not do.
And I'll keep everyone in this guessing loop,
Till you're sick of your own mental stew.

Neither my love nor my heartbreak
Will have any credit takers.
You see I've truly failed as a romantic,
Because I'm a serial mischief maker.

12. Navy Blue Vendetta

When you're at your worst
And in your most shattered state,
I know you'll dream of exacting a revenge
That is both bloodthirsty and passionate.
But let me remind you instead
That true revenge is cold and calculated.

I know you lead with your heart,
So everything is tinged with red,
But just this once, you'll need to
Rely blindly on your head.
Trust me, alright? and we'll
Quickly put this matter to bed.

The warrior fights with a sword,
And loses some of his own blood too.
But do you know the one who loses nothing
And rather lets his interest accrue?
The accountant who picks up their pen
Because they know real vendetta is navy-blue.

The accountant knows their books,
Every line, every cent, and every clue.
There's no space for a careless mistake,

No margin for an error to slip through.
And when the numbers don't quite add up,
You'll know—the reckoning is long overdue.

And when they extract their pound of flesh,
That's the real time for terror.
A silent debt, a patient wait—
No time left for mercy, trial, or error.
For vengeance is never in a moment's heat
But always in the weight of a well-timed ledger.

True revenge is a waiting game,
A breath held, a smile feigned oh-so-wide.
You let them think they've walked away,
With no price to pay and no need to hide.
But the day their guard is finally down,
Show them their place with ruthless pride.

Now's not the time for embellishments,
For you must strike once and strike hard.
Forget about pulling out the knives,
Just use a single glass shard.
You know what would now be perfect?
Taking out the piece they'd lodged in your heart.

And when you do, it must be swift,
So sharp, so final, so precise.

Because you should dirty your hands just once.
Never again should they be allowed to rise.
For when the accountant comes to collect,
Even the gambler is wary of rolling his dice.
This is a true lesson inked in navy blue,
Yet forever etched in their vice.

13. Limitless Love

Everything passes
But love will stay.
There will be moments
When it won't feel that way,
And love may take a different shape or form
Than what it looked like yesterday
But that is all okay.

Sometimes,
Love will even make you walk away.
And you'll wonder if you were
Actually supposed to stay?
But remember, when it comes to true love
You won't be able to walk too far.
There is no escaping the fact
That it's what you truly are.

14. Alchemy

Let's take our pain
And spin it into gold.
Tell our story before
It gathers mould.
I know these stories and patterns
Seem generationally old.
But someone needs to break them
For which you have to be bold.
Yes, while exposing your wounds
You may feel like your heart is getting sold.
But the fire in you can, and will,
Always survive the societal cold.
So now, no matter what
You are repeatedly told,
Remember you are the ace
And everybody else will have to fold.
Stay in your truth and slowly,
This is the standard your world will learn to hold.

15. Poetic Complexities

I've often questioned if
Painful poetry should even be written?
It's like harbouring a pet-snake
And then asking to be bitten.
Why should such magnificent
Literary monuments be raised
To mark the horrors and
Memories you'd prefer erased?
And then comes the most obsessive,
The most bone-chilling thought.
What if by writing so much,
You're perpetuating your worst karmic knot?
What if your words end up hurting
Those who first hurt you,
And by doing this,
You're ensuring your destiny is through.

But honestly, as painful as poetry is,
It is also, at heart, deeply kind.
It is never about blaming others,
It's about releasing them and finding peace of mind.
And sometimes these monuments don't mark pain
But rather your most important lessons learned.

Remember, you have to build these bridges
Before they can finally be burned.

16. Legacies of Softness

I think even before love
With someone else can start,
We must practice how to
Consistently hold our own heart.
At least once, we must allow ourselves
To be deeply moved by art
And we must happily embrace our mortal stupidity,
Before considering ourselves smart.

Sometimes we over-water roots,
And forget to spray some on the flower.
We strive to blaze like the sun
And forget the relief brought on by a shower
We harden too much looking at mountains
And forget water too has immense power.
We force ourselves to be very brave,
When occasionally, it is practical to cower.

Too often, we sideline simplicity
In our bid to be absolutely legendary.
We ignore what's happening currently
By mercilessly chasing an eternity.
And ever stuck in our cranial complexity,
We truly forget: *there is no immortality.*

So instead of getting wrapped up in all this intricacy

Can we simply start by making softness our genuine
legacy?

17. A Shared Voice

For too long,
Women have learned to hold their silence.
To keep their voices suppressed
So they don't end up looking like tyrants.
Tirelessly, we adapt to social cues.
Are always mindful of our p's and q's.
And never would we dream of hurting another,
Even if it means we don't say what is cuttingly true.

But generations of unconscious trauma
Are hard to override
When labels of shrillness and hysteria
Overcrowd our side.
Together, how do we even begin to stitch,
The brutal strangulation of an ancestral witch,
With the shockingly modern accusation
Of being "such a bitch"?

It's so hard to even begin to try.
I think, first we all need to have a good collective cry.
And only then can we go on to wonder why,
Is it that we're afraid to speak up
Or are we just innately shy?

Let's be gentle with ourselves
If we decide to speak up one day,
And realise, much to our dismay,
That even before uttering a single word,
Self-doubt has taken our breath away.

When our words are still learning to sprout,
There's still some time,
Before we can absolutely rail and shout.
So, in the meanwhile,
Why not help a sister out?

Tell me your story,
And I'll tell you mine.
However each one shapes the retelling
Is absolutely fine.

For soon, we'll understand,
Our stories are mostly the same,
Barring a few characters
And the heroine's name.

And through this
Shared story,
We'll learn that none of us
Has a reason to be sorry

Except for the time
We try to make each other feel small.
Because women fighting women,
Is the most painful root of it all.

And after centuries of our collective pain,
When we're faced with the realisation,
That we've already lost more than we stand to gain,

Even then,
In choosing to listen to
Each other's most authentic voice,
We come together to make healing
Our most significant and united choice.

18. Compulsive Closure

Sometimes,

When a chapter closes abruptly,

The fact that it ended

Is all the truth

You really need.

Compulsively seek more

And soon you'll struggle to breath.

Come, I'll give you the hardest advice

You'll ever receive:

"Stop chasing closure,

When erasure is what your heart silently pleads."

19. Hard Truths

Stop it.
Just stop believing that
You are a victim of fate.
It's nothing but a convenient excuse
For you to sit around and wait,
As you hand over the reigns of a
Destiny that was always yours to make.

20. Soft Truths

You'll never fully be heartbroken
If you truly understand love.

Should your outside romantic bubble ever burst,
Recognise that it doesn't matter
For love is always within you first.

If you truly see yourself as
Love's original source,
Then your path will be sprinkled with miracles
Just waiting to unfold,
For love moves things that can't
Even be touched by any other force.

21. Advice To the Good Girl

As a good girl, we know your love and compassion
Is not up for negotiation,
But for the time being, we'll let that slide.
When they call you to the table,
Walk in with your head completely sorted and stable,
Further armed with your irreproachable pride.

First, they'll offer you their condescension,
Belittling you and hoping you'll run or hide.
Pay no heed to the vacuum of their words—
Their chiding means nothing, just let it subside.

It's not that they don't know your worth,
It's simply because that's something
You often let yourself and others override.
So now they'll pull out their sharpest arrow
And cloak it with honeyed praise, thinking
This is how to sway your goody-goody side.

For a moment, you might stumble, you might waver,
But catch yourself before you're tied.
And if not a single thing they offer
Is what you want, what feels just and right—

Then simply walk away.
Walk away with a lion's stride.
They'll guilt you that saying 'no' is an act of rebellion,
But know that it is your genuine birthright.

22. Flood

You're so used to her
Effortless flow,
That I doubt her depth is something
You've ever tried to know.

You take a coin
And chuck it bang into her heart,
Then you choke her with the ashes
Of the ones who have come to depart.

Later, as supplication,
You offer her floating lights and flowers,
Thinking all this while,
Generosity and mercy are her truest powers.

Unclothed, you submerge in her,
Hoping she'll accept every inch of you.
But when it's time for her to reveal her true self,
What is it that you do?

When she decides to rise,
You start to cower.
This is not done. You bathed in her softness.
Now you must drown in her glower.

23. Less is More

When the weight
Of phrasing the perfect poetic encore
From your remnant free-floating emotions
Leaves you helplessly exhausted and sore,
Know that
One honest poem
Is worth so much more
Than all the countless books
Lining up the shelves at a store.